101 Cool Pool Games
for Children

Dedication

This book is affectionately dedicated to the following people for all of their endless support: my husband, Guy; my children, Andrew and Addison, who taught me the importance of play; Brittany, Sierra, Tyler, Jordan, and Gianna Bella June; my parents, Bud and Judy Hanson; and my friend Irene Gallo Murphy.

SmartFun Books from Hunter House

101 Music Games for Children by Jerry Storms
101 More Music Games for Children by Jerry Storms
101 Dance Games for Children by Paul Rooyackers
101 More Dance Games for Children by Paul Rooyackers
101 Drama Games for Children by Paul Rooyackers
101 More Drama Games for Children by Paul Rooyackers
101 Movement Games for Children by Huberta Wiertsema
101 Language Games for Children by Paul Rooyackers
101 Improv Games for Children by Bob Bedore
101 Life Skills Games for Children by Bernie Badegruber
101 More Life Skills Games for Children by Bernie Badegruber
101 Cool Pool Games for Children by Kim Rodomista
101 Family Vacation Games by Shando Varda
101 Relaxation Games for Children by Allison Bartl
101 Quick-Thinking Games + Riddles for Children by Allison Bartl
101 Pep-Up Games for Children by Allison Bartl
404 Deskside Activities for Energetic Kids by Barbara Davis, MA, MFA
Yoga Games for Children by Danielle Bersma and Marjoke Visscher
The Yoga Adventure for Children by Helen Purperhart
Yoga Exercises for Teens by Helen Purperhart
The Yoga Zoo Adventure by Helen Purperhart

Ordering

Trade bookstores in the U.S. and Canada please contact:
Publishers Group West
1700 Fourth St., Berkeley CA 94710
Phone: (800) 788-3123   Fax: (800) 351-5073

Hunter House books are available at bulk discounts for textbook course adoptions; to qualifying community, health care, and government organizations; and for special promotions and fund-raising. For details please contact:

Special Sales Department
Hunter House Inc., PO Box 2914, Alameda CA 94501-0914
Phone: (510) 865-5282   Fax: (510) 865-4295
E-mail: ordering@hunterhouse.com

Individuals can order our books from most bookstores, by calling
(800) 266-5592, or from our website at **www.hunterhouse.com**

1̲0̲1

Cool Pool Games

FOR

Children

Fun and Fitness for Swimmers
of All Levels

Kim Rodomista

A Hunter House SmartFun Book

Hunter House Inc., Publishers
PO Box 2914
Alameda CA 94501-0914

Library of Congress Cataloging-in-Publication Data

Rodomista, Kim.
    101 cool pool games for children : fun and fitness for swimmers of all levels / Kim Rodomista.
        p. cm. — (A Hunter House smartfun book)
    Includes index.
    ISBN-13: 978-0-89793-483-1 (pbk.)
    ISBN-10: 0-89793-483-0 (pbk.)
    ISBN-13: 978-0-89793-484-8 (sp.)
    ISBN-10: 0-89793-484-9 (sp.)
1. Swimming for children. 2. Swimming pools. 3. Games. I. Title. II. Title: One hundred one cool pool games for children. III. Title: One hundred and one cool pool games for children. IV. Series.
GV837.2.R63 2006
797.2'1083—dc22   2006015693

Project Credits

Cover Design: Jil Weil & Stefanie Gold
Illustrations: Robin Patterson
Book Production: Stefanie Gold
Developmental and Copy Editor: Christy Steele
Proofreader: Herman Leung
Acquisitions Editor: Jeanne Brondino
Editor: Alexandra Mummery
Customer Service Manager: Christina Sverdrup
Order Fulfillment: Washul Lakdhon
Administrator: Theresa Nelson
Computer Support: Peter Eichelberger
Publisher: Kiran S. Rana

Printed and bound by Sheridan Books, Ann Arbor, Michigan
Manufactured in the United States of America

9 8 7 6 5 4 3   First Edition   11 12 13 14 15

Contents

A detailed list of the games indicating water skill level needed
begins on the next page.

List of Games

Preface

Everybody in the world is intimately connected to water. It doesn't matter whether a person lives in a desert or along an ocean coast; we all started life the same way—swimming in our mother's womb. These early memories are most likely stored somewhere in the unconscious mind. So it's no wonder that many children and adults enjoy the sensation of floating and moving through water.

As enjoyable as water recreation can be, if approached with a purpose and a plan it becomes even more than a refreshing way to relax. Playing structured water games is a fun way to help children develop social skills and keep them healthy. Just add water and this book will provide family and friends with 101 of the coolest pool games.

A child doesn't have to be an expert swimmer to benefit from water play. This book provides games for all skill levels; so whether a child is just learning how to swim or if he is the next Michael Phelps, there are games for everyone. Enjoy!

— Kim Rodomista
April 2006

For easy reading we have alternated use of the male and female pronouns. Of course, every "he" also includes "she," and vice versa.

Introduction

Why Choose Water Play?

Water is for more than splashing! Adding structured physical activity to water recreation doesn't diminish the fun, yet helps children develop health benefits that last a lifetime. The water play ideas in *101 Cool Pool Games* provide children with an enjoyable way to burn calories, improve the cardiovascular system, and enhance their overall fitness level.

Water itself is like a piece of exercise equipment. It provides about twelve times the resistance of air, making any movement in water an effective exercise. In addition, water provides both buoyancy and support for the body. As people move deeper in water, they weigh less. As a result, people can exercise in water with far less impact stress on their body's joints, bones, and muscles. This makes water play ideal for children and adults of all sizes and fitness levels.

Water play provides many social benefits, too. Learning new games develops children's listening skills and cognitive development. Games also provide a supportive environment to help children, even shy ones, enhance their interpersonal skills. Successfully interacting with others helps them acquire self-confidence. Additionally, games that require children to use their imagination encourage participants to express their ideas and share their creativity with others.

How to Use This Book

Role of the Leader

Games are more successful when one person is in charge. The leader has many responsibilities, including supervising the game. When designating a leader, there are some important factors to consider. The leader should be mature, ideally an adult or one of the older players. In addition, given the nature of these games, the leader should be a strong swimmer.

The leader must be someone who is fair to all players. One of the leader's tasks is dividing the teams in an equitable way for all of the players. He or she also keeps score, tracks time, and referees when needed.

The leader should also be a good communicator. He or she must clearly explain the rules of each game, the use of the props, and show the players the starting line and finishing line. The leader may need to calmly arbitrate disputes among players. In addition, sometimes children become upset when they don't win. The leader should be ready with a pep talk for these unhappy occasions.

Finally, the leader should know the players and their skill levels. Any game can be modified by the leader to suit the age group and skill level of the children. The leader can decide if the winner of the racing game is the slowest or the fastest swimmer, or the most creative, bravest, or funniest player.

Safety

Before the kids enter the water, important safety considerations must be addressed. Please review pool safety rules with each child before beginning any game.

The following precautions will help create a safe environment for water play:

- Always maintain a high adult to child ratio. The younger the children, the more adult supervisors needed.
- Always supervise children when they are in the pool. **Never** leave them alone. In only a few seconds even the most experienced swimmer may encounter an in-water emergency that requires adult assistance.
- Minimize diving and jumping into the pool.
- Minimize pushing and rough play.
- Do not allow "dunking."
- Let all the children know if there is a deep end of the pool and where the pool begins to deepen.
- Remember that inflatable swim aids are not suitable lifesaving devices. Do not rely on them to keep children safe. If you aren't sure about someone's swimming ability, watch them closely to make sure they stay in the shallow water.
- Some of these games require running in the pool. So it is best if the children wear rubber-soled shoes in the pool to prevent them from slipping.
- Make sure the children drink liquids to stay hydrated.
- Protect children's skin with waterproof sun block lotion.

Some games may not be suitable for all children. As mentioned above, to safeguard the safety of all participants, it is important to know the age group and swimming skill level of the players. Each game has an icon that shows the recommended skill level. Please consider the icons and the directions when selecting games. Then use your judgment to choose safe, appropriate games for the players.

Selecting the Games

The games in this book are organized into seven sections, each with a unique purpose: Imagination Games, Tag Games, Individual Games, Team Games, Out-of-the-Pool Games, Racing Games, and Water Exercises. The games are grouped into a section by their main focus.

Each of the pool games can stand alone. However, you can also structure a water play session by selecting several games from different sections of this book. When planning a water play session, keep in mind any time constraints. It's often best to plan more games than there may be time to play. This way, the children won't run out of things to do. Some of the water play games, such as Marco Polo (Game #19), can last a very long time. Consider putting time limitations on some of these games to create additional challenge and excitement.

Carefully plan the variety and order of the selected games to meet the following goals: to keep the time fun and to be sensitive to the different physical abilities of each child. Varying the kinds of games keeps water play interesting. Varying the intensity of games keeps water play inclusive for those at different levels of fitness.

Stretching is an important first step to do before playing any of the pool games. The stretches in the Water Exercises section on page 117 will help prepare muscles for physical activity and reduce the risk of injury. Some games are more physically challenging than others. Consider beginning with less strenuous games and progressing to more challenging ones.

For instance, you may begin with a water exercise stretch as a warm-up. Then slowly raise the physical activity level with an imagination game. Raise the intensity level further with an individual or team game. Next, a racing game would be even more physically challenging. You could prolong the cardiovascular benefits by inserting another water exercise. Consider adding an out-of-the-pool game for rest or to occupy children who have been eliminated. Then cool down with another imagination game.

There are hundreds of ways to combine the games and use the ideas in this book. We invite you to be creative.

Number of Players

When choosing a game, consider the number of players and adjust the game as needed. The number of players can tremendously affect a game. A tag game is more fun with five players than it is with two players; if there are only two players, look for games recommended for smaller groups. A racing game may become chaotic with fifty-five players. In this situation, perhaps divide the group into smaller groups or several teams. If a large group is playing a tag game, more than one person may be designated as "It."

Type of Pool and Space Needed

These games can be safely played in any type of water. I have played these games in Lake Winnipesaukee and the Atlantic Ocean!

The space and size of pool needed for each game varies. Although many games can be played in any type of water, read the game's directions carefully to determine if a certain type of pool is necessary and the amount of space needed around the pool.

Preparation

Each game's directions describe any preparatory tasks the leader must do. Most games require no special preparation. Others, however, require the leader to set up goals, choose beginning and finish lines, or gather props. Props used in some of the games include: beach balls, coins, hula hoops, water balloons, buckets, cups with holes, garden hose, plastic two-liter bottles, empty milk jugs with caps, plastic pool rings, ping-pong balls, sponges, squirt guns, plastic figures or dolls, net, long ropes, kickboard, squirt bottles, noodles, foam discs, rafts, plastic baseball bat, beach balls, and a toy called a toypedo.

Be sure to have plenty of towels and drinks, too.

Key to the Icons Used in the Games

To help you find games suitable for a particular situation, the games are coded with symbols or icons. These icons tell you, at a glance, the following things about the game:

- The size of the group needed
- The level of skill needed
- If props are required
- If physical contact is or might be involved

These icons are explained in more detail below. Two icons included in other SmartFun books (age level and time) have been omitted here because the games are categorized by water skill level needed rather than age level and because the duration of each game will vary depending on a number of factors, including the size of the group, the physical activity involved, the time limit set by the leader, variations or modifications made by the leader, and whether or not the particular game appeals to the players.

The size of the group needed. There are games in this book for groups of all sizes, from individuals to large teams. If a game requires a large number of players or groups of a specific size, the game will be marked with the appropriate icon:

 = Suitable for a large group to play together

 = Suitable for a group of any size

 = Requires an even number of players

 = Requires 2 or more children (and so on)

Note: Although we have included the "even number" icon for many games, many of them can also be played by an odd number of players if the leader makes slight modifications (e.g., if one player goes twice, if the leader joins in, etc.). We include the icon simply to suggest the ideal group composition.

The level of skill needed. Each game has a recommended skill level and is marked with the designated icon.

All players. Appropriate for children with or without swimming abilities. They must be able to understand simple directions. The games in this book suited to players of all skill levels are marked with the following icon:

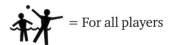 = For all players

Beginning players. Children who are learning how to swim; they can float, but are unable to put their head under water. The games in this book suited to beginning players are marked with the following icon:

 = For beginning players

Intermediate players. Children who are able to swim at least 10 feet and are comfortable floating, going under water, and jumping in the pool. The games in this book suited to intermediate players are marked with the following icon:

 = For intermediate players

Advanced players. Children who have mastered all types of swimming strokes and can swim under water or in any depth of water; they can dive or jump into the deep end of the pool. The games in this book suited to advanced players are marked with the following icon:

 = For advanced players

If props are required. Many of the games require no special props. In some cases, though, items such as beach balls, water balloons, kickboards, or other materials are integral to running and playing a game. Games requiring props are flagged with the icon below, and the necessary materials are listed under the Props heading. Note that optional props will also be flagged.

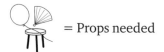 = Props needed

If physical contact is or might be involved. Although a certain amount of body contact might be acceptable in certain environments, the following icon has been inserted at the top of any games that might involve anything from a small amount of contact to minor collisions. You can figure out in advance if the game is suitable for your participants and/or environment.

 = Physical contact likely

Imagination Games

Albert Einstein once said, "Imagination is more important than knowledge." Yet, since imagination is hard to quantify as an "achievement," in today's success-driven world many people discount the importance of imagination to a child's development.

Even so, imagination—the art of dreaming, inventing, and improvising—is as important today as it was in Einstein's time. Through imagination, children learn to experiment with different roles. Through imaginative play, they are given a safe environment to express their inner thoughts and feelings. Over time, scientists believe that imaginative self-expression leads children to better handle their emotions.

So toss the bathing caps; thinking caps are mandatory for these games. Each one allows players to explore their unique imagination through water play. This style of game can be easily adapted to accommodate all skill levels.

Imagination Games

Follow the Leader

How to Play: Almost everybody has played Follow the Leader at some point. This game is exactly like the old favorite, but with a twist—it's played in the water! This is a great game to get younger children comfortable with the water.

Players stand in a circle with plenty of space in the middle. Each player selects a type of movement. The players can select any type of movement or create an imaginative movement of their own. If a player cannot think of a movement, the leader can offer suggestions.

Next, the first player moves into the center of the circle. He performs his chosen movement. Everybody else copies his movement. Soon, everyone should be doing the same thing.

Players continue doing the movement for a set amount of time or until the leader calls for a switch. Then, the next player takes a turn in the center of the circle. That player does a new movement. Players take turns until everyone has performed a movement in the center of the circle.

Examples

- Leaping
- Blow bubbles
- Splash
- Go under water
- Running
- Jumping
- Hopping on one leg
- Marching

Variations

- More advanced players can travel around the pool as part of their movement. For example, they could move from corner to corner, zigzag, forward, backward, or sideways.
- This game can be played as Simon Says, too. In this variation, the players should take turns being "Simon." "Simon" goes into the middle of the circle and instructs the players which movements to do. Players should do the movements only if the designated "Simon" says, "Simon says…" before performing the movement. Any player who is tricked into doing the movement without hearing "Simon says…" is eliminated from the game.

What Did You Say?

How to Play: This game's original name is the Telephone Game. With water added, it becomes What Did You Say?

The players stand in a circle. The leader thinks of a word or a short sentence. Next, the leader and the person to the right go under water. The leader then says the word to this player. Each player will repeat the same word (under water), or the word they think they have heard, to the next person in line.

The round ends when the word comes back to the original leader. The leader then announces the last underwater word to the group (above the water). If that was not the original word, the leader reveals the correct word. The leader can continue the game as long as the kids stay interested.

3

Spell It Out

How to Play: No, this game is not a spelling bee contest, but children do have to spell a word with their bodies!

Divide the group into two teams. Choose a time limit for forming a word in the water and guessing the word. Also, set a point limit to end the game.

Team 1 gets into the water, and the other team waits on the side of the pool. Players work together to choose a short, simple word. After the word is chosen, the players use their bodies to form the word as quickly as possible. They move their arms, legs, and other body parts in the shape of letters while floating on top of the water. If they form a readable word in the time frame (as judged by the leader), the team receives a point.

The members of Team 2 then try to guess what the word is within a designated period of time. If they guess correctly, they receive a point.

Next, Team 2 takes a turn in the water to spell out a word. Team 1 tries to guess the word. Turns alternate in this manner. The game ends when the teams reach the point limit set by the leader, usually 10 points.

Examples of words

NO	*ZOO*
YES	*SIT*
POP	*IT*
WE	*TELL*
TOP	*OUT*
LOVE	*KISS*
LOT	*CAT*

What Am I?

How to Play: Just like in the game of charades, this game requires some thought. This is especially true since this game is played in the water. Divide the group into two teams. Each team must create a list of ideas to act out. The leader may give some guidelines or suggestions to help teams focus on creating a list, such as all animals or all cartoon characters. Then each team gives their list to the leader. Each player will receive an idea from the opposite team's list to act out.

Each player takes a turn. First, the leader selects an idea for the player. Then the player acts out the idea for her team. She tries to help her team guess what she is in the shortest period of time, but she can't say the word out loud. If the team members guess correctly, they get a point. Then, the next team takes a turn.

The game continues like this for a set amount of time or until a predetermined point limit is reached.

Examples

- Dolphin
- Frog
- Fish
- Ship
- Raft
- Snake
- Car
- Whale

Variation: This game can also be played by individuals, instead of a team. When played this way, the leader makes up the ideas, and only 2 players are necessary—one to act out the idea and one to guess what it is. No score is kept in this variation.

On with the Show

Props: Beach balls; rafts; music (optional)—be creative!

How to Play: I enjoy watching synchronized swimming in the Olympics, but it's hilarious to watch a group of kids putting on their own synchronized-swimming program. Get the video camera ready! Depending on the number of players, the leader can divide them into groups or allow them to be in one group.

Allow the group to be creative in planning a routine. Select the props and music. Ribbons can be given to the most creative, the silliest, etc.

Examples

- Jumping jacks
- Pop out of the water
- Run in place
- Float on back with a leg lift
- Handstands
- Run forward

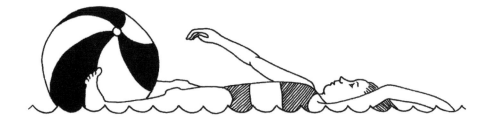

Tag Games

Tag games help increase fitness by using fun-filled physical activity to keep children moving. If a strenuous tag game lasts for fifteen minutes or more, it becomes aerobic activity and improves cardiovascular health.

Another benefit of tag games is their versatility. They can be adapted to suit the needs of different sized groups. A tag game can be fun with five players or twenty-five players. For large groups, tag games can be divided into smaller groups or several teams. Or a leader can designate more than one player as "It."

Each of these tag games could last a very long time. The leader's role is to determine when the game will end. The leader may enforce a time limit or end the game only if the children seem to be tired or losing interest.

When planning to play tag, keep in mind the game's rules. If it requires elimination, occupy the kids on the sidelines with an out-of-the-pool activity or game.

Car Tag

How to Play: Divide the players into pairs. One is a car, and the other is the driver. The car may walk or swim, but she must hold her hands out in front of her body with her eyes closed. Drivers keep their eyes open. They steer the cars by standing behind their partners and placing their hands on their partners' shoulders.

One car and its driver are chosen to be "It." As in the traditional game of tag, the person who is "It" tries to tag another player. In this game, cars only tag cars. Drivers avoid getting their cars tagged by carefully maneuvering them around other cars.

When the "It" car tags another car, the tagged car's team becomes the new "It." Cars and drivers switch roles, and the game continues.

Lifeguard Tag

How to Play: Designate one player to be the lifeguard. Divide the other players into two teams. Each team must move to opposite sides of the pool.

The lifeguard calls the names of two players, one from each team. These two players must swim and exchange places before the lifeguard tags one of them. If someone is tagged, he becomes the next lifeguard. If no one is tagged, the lifeguard calls the names of two more players.

Tag Games

Jellyfish Bite

How to Play: Choose one player to be the jellyfish, or chaser. The other players must scatter around the pool. The jellyfish tries to tag any other player on the foot, knee, or other spot that is difficult to hold. This tag is like a jellyfish sting. The person tagged becomes the next jellyfish. Depending on where the player was tagged, he must hop, limp, or swim with one arm while chasing the next victim. No biting please!

Racing Sea Rays

How to Play: Group players together in pairs. Choose one pair to be the sea rays. Ask everyone else to stand in a circle and hold one of their partner's hands.

The sea rays, who should also hold hands, move around the outer circle. When they are ready, they choose another pair and touch them on the shoulders. The tagged pair must step out of the circle and run or swim around the outer circle in the opposite direction of the sea rays while still holding hands. Both groups try to get back into the empty space first. The pair that makes it to the empty spot last becomes the sea rays for the next round.

Tag Games

The Blob

How to Play: This is a fun and funny game. Designate one person to be the "Blob." Everyone else swims around the pool, trying not to be tagged. If a swimmer is tagged, he or she must join hands with the "Blob" and continue to try and tag others. When other players are tagged, they must join the "Blob," too. Finally, there is only one player left. The player left is the winner and the next "Blob"!

11

Tag Games

Underwater Tag

How to Play: Choose one person to be the chaser. Everyone else swims around the pool. To avoid the chaser, the players must go under water; the chaser can tag only a body part that is above the water. As long as the players are under water they are safe, but when they surface for air, they are back in the game. If a player is tagged, she must get out of the pool until the game is over.

The game ends when all the players are tagged or at a designated time set by the leader. Then, a new person takes a turn as the chaser.

Hook On

How to Play: Players form a single line by holding on to each other's hands. The last person in line tries to tag the first person in line. To prevent this, the first person moves around the pool swinging the line from side to side. When the first person is tagged, the end person goes to the front of the line, and everyone moves down one space in line.

Variation: To make this game more challenging, allow only the first and last player to have their feet touching the bottom of the pool. All other players must stay in a tucked position as they are being pulled around the pool.

Tag Games

Moby Dick

How to Play: Choose one player to be "Moby Dick." The other players are the fish. Have "Moby Dick" float on his back. The other fish gather around the whale.

When "Moby Dick" suddenly yells, "Thar she blows," the fish start to swim away, and Moby Dick quickly turns over and swims to capture one of the fish. If no fish is tagged within one minute, the game repeats itself. If "Moby Dick" tags a fish, the fish becomes the next "Moby Dick."

Tag Games

Elbow Tag

How to Play: All players get in the water. Designate one player to be the chaser and one to be the runner. All other players must have a partner. Each player must link elbows with her partner to form a pair.

Next, the chaser tries to tag the runner. The runner may seek safety by hooking his elbow to the elbow of someone in a pair, so the paired players should try to avoid the runner by moving around the pool. If a paired player has her elbow hooked by the runner, the other member of the pair immediately becomes the new runner.

When a chaser tags a runner, the two reverse roles for a new round of play.

 large group

Tag Games

Fish and Net

How to Play: Five players are chosen to be the net, while others are fish. The fish scatter around the swimming pool. The five players link hands to create a "net."

The game leader calls out, "Swim, fish, swim." At this time, the net players move around the pool, trying to capture as many fish as they can by touching them. The fish try to swim from the net. The fish may swim underwater to avoid getting caught. If a fish is caught, he must sit on the side of the pool until the game is finished.

After all the fish are caught, or a set amount of time determined by the leader passes, five different players are chosen to form the net.

The King's Bridge

How to Play: Designate one player to be the king or queen. This player will stand on the deck of the pool with his or her back to the other players. The other players stand in the water against the opposite wall of the pool. The players in the water call out, "King _____" or "Queen _____" (insert the child's name), may we cross your bridge?"

The king or queen will reply, "Only if you are _____ (let the child choose the category)." The players fitting into that category may safely cross over to the opposite side of the pool.

The players who are left behind must wait for the king or queen to say, "Go," at which point the king or queen jumps into the pool. The players who are left behind try to swim across the pool without being tagged. The first player who is tagged becomes the next king or queen. If nobody is tagged, the same person is king or queen again.

Examples

- Only if you are wearing blue
- Only if you are a boy/girl
- Only if your first/last name begins with (insert letter)
- Only if your hair is (insert color)
- Only if your birthday is in (insert month)

Tag Games

Marco Polo

How to Play: Designate one player to be "Marco." Everyone else will scatter around the pool. "Marco" must close her eyes and count to ten. Next, "Marco," who has to keep her eyes closed, begins to search for the other players by saying, "Marco."

The other players swim around the pool, and they must shout "Polo" whenever they hear "Marco." By listening carefully, "Marco" must try to find and tag another player, who then becomes the new "Marco."

18

Tag Games

Pirate Treasure

Props: A coin

How to Play: The leader should decide where to locate the goal and then designate one player to be the pirate. The pirate receives a coin to hold. Everyone else stands in a line. They place their cupped hands underwater with their thumbs facing up.

The pirate walks down the line. The pirate may pretend to put the coin in someone's hand or may really drop the coin into a player's hand. The person receiving the coin must swim or run to the goal without being tagged by other players. The pirate cannot tag the player. If a player who receives the coin is tagged, he returns to being a player. If he makes it to the goal, he becomes the pirate.

Tag Games

Ship and Barnacles

How to Play: Unlike most tag games, when it is usually more fun being "It," this game is more fun being a barnacle!

Choose the strongest swimmer to be "It," or the ship. Everyone else will be a barnacle. Then, the ship moves around the pool trying to tag a barnacle. When it does, the barnacle must attach itself to the ship, but the barnacles' feet must be off the bottom of the pool. Now the ship and its attached barnacle must try to tag other barnacles. Usually the ship runs out of energy before all the barnacles are attached. Then someone else takes a turn as the ship. The ship that succeeds in attaching the most barnacles wins!

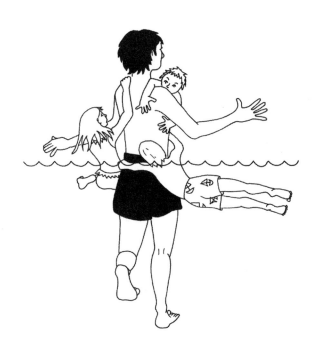

Tag Games

Turtle Tag

How to Play: Designate one player to be the chaser. Everyone else must swim around the pool. The chaser tries to tag other players. If a player is tagged, she must turn over and float on her back! She must stay this way until a player who has not been tagged touches her. Then she is free to swim again.

The game ends if everyone is tagged. This can take a long time or may never happen, so the leader may want to set a time limit. This will give other players a chance to be the chaser.

21

Tag Games

Piranha Tag

How to Play: This game is a reverse tag game, and it moves very fast. Designate the victim. All of the other players are piranhas.

Allow the victim to swim away from the other players. On the leader's signal, the piranhas try to tag the victim. The piranha who tags the victim now becomes the victim and must quickly swim away from the other piranhas. The victim who was just tagged by a piranha, however, cannot immediately turn around and tag the new victim back—instead, he must allow the new victim at least five seconds to swim away before starting to chase her.

Freeze Tag

How to Play: Choose one person to be "It." The other players try to run away. If a player is tagged, he must freeze. The only way to thaw or unfreeze him is for another player to swim between his legs. The game ends when everybody is frozen at one time. Since this takes a very long time to achieve, the leader may want to specify the amount of time each player can be "It." This will ensure that everyone has a turn.

Variation: To make this game more challenging, once a player is tagged she must freeze in a suspended position (feet must not be touching the bottom of the pool). Another player must swim underneath her to unfreeze her.

Tag Games

Shark and Minnows

How to Play: Designate one player to be the shark; the shark must stand in the middle of the pool. All the other players are minnows and must stand along the edge of the pool.

The shark yells out, "Minnows!" Then the minnows jump into the water. They try to swim to the other side without being tagged by the shark. The minnows that make it can get out of the water again. If they are tagged, they become sharks and must stay in the water. Then, to begin the next round, all the sharks call out, "Minnows!"

The game continues until there is only one minnow left. This minnow is the winner and starts as the shark in the next game.

Tag Games

Bridges and Canals

How to Play: Choose one person to be the caller. Ask the caller to stand on the deck of the pool. The other players go in the pool. They form parallel rows of about six players each. The players in each row stand an arm's length away from each other and hold hands with their arms extended. When players face front (toward the caller), the aisles between rows are bridges. When they turn right, the aisles between rows are canals.

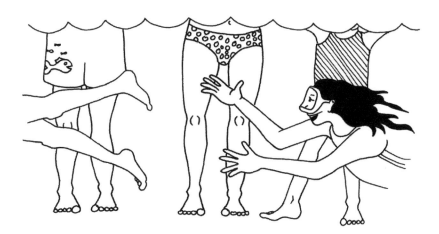

Select two players. One will be the runner, and the other will be the chaser. As the game begins, all players face front and remain holding hands with the people in their row. On the signal, the chaser pursues the runner down the bridges by swimming or running. At anytime, the caller may shout, "Canals!" Then the players turn right and take the hands of new neighbors. No one may swim under or through the clasped hands.

After three minutes, if the runner is not caught, the leader can call the game a draw and designate a new runner and chaser.

Snatch the Bait

Props: Some small item that be held in a player's hand as "bait"

How to Play: Divide the players into two teams. One team will receive the bait and hide it behind the back of a teammate. To fool the opposing team, each player should have their hands behind their backs. Once the bait is hidden, each team lines up against the side of the pool facing the other team.

On the leader's signal, members of the team with the bait attempt to bring it to the opposite side of the pool without the person who is holding it getting tagged. If the opposing team tags a player without the bait, that player is out. If the player with the bait makes it to the opposite side, their team earns a point and the ability to hide the bait—and potentially score—in the next round. If the player with the bait is tagged, neither team scores, but the tagging team receives the bait for the next round.

Individual Games

This type of game works well with small groups or younger players. The physical activity required in the games helps them to develop their motor skills and reflexes. Moving through the water helps to build muscle strength and endurance. And as children have fun exploring their individual abilities, they also gain a new level of self-confidence and a desire to achieve.

The leader can choose whether or not to have a "winner" for each game. The "winner" does not have to be linked to performance, such as the "fastest" or the "best," with this style of game. I recommend originality when handing out the awards. For example, some awards could be: "The Sneakiest," "The Scariest," "The Slowest," or "The Most Creative." This way, every child participating can be a winner in some way.

Individual Games

Limbo

Props: Pole; jump rope or hula-hoop; music (optional)

Most people have played this game once or twice, but I bet most haven't played this game in the pool! It's harder.

How to Play: Players form a line. Start with the pole at the surface of the water. Each person takes a turn swimming under the pole. Any player who touches the pole, with any body part, is eliminated. After each round, move the pole a little lower, until only one person is left.

Variation: Start the game by placing the pole low under the water. Each player must go under the pole when it is under the water. After each round, move the pole higher. When the pole is brought out of the water, the players must jump over the pole.

Individual Games

Jump, You, Jump!

Props: Pole or noodle with string and a gummy fish or gummy worm attached to it. Instead of gummies, a ribbon can be tied to the end of the pole.

How to Play: Designate one player to hold the fishing pole. This person stands on the side of the pool and dangles the string with the prop attached over the water. The other players try to jump and grab the prop at the end of the string.

The person who can jump the highest out of the water and grab the "fish" wins.

Penny Hunt

Props: Pennies or other coins

How to Play: All players stand on the deck of the pool with their backs toward the water. The leader then throws pennies into the pool. On the leader's signal, the players turn around and jump in the water to search for the pennies. The player who collects the most pennies is the winner.

Variation: Paint some of the pennies white; this makes the pennies more difficult to find.

Red Light, Green Light

How to Play: Choose one person to be the stoplight. (It's a good idea for an adult to be the stoplight first, especially if the children haven't played the game before.) All the other players line up side by side across the pool. The stoplight then turns his back and shouts, "Green light!" Then the players run as fast as they can in the water toward him. When the stoplight yells, "Red light!" he turns around and tries to catch the other players in motion.

Anyone caught moving is eliminated. The object is to reach the stoplight without getting caught moving. The stoplight starts the action again by turning his back and shouting, "Green light!"

The game proceeds until a player tags the stoplight and becomes "It" for the next game. If all the players are called out, the stoplight wins. If this happens, the stoplight gets to be "It" again.

Underwater Race

How to Play: Players line up against one end of the pool wall. On a signal, everyone goes under water and pushes off the wall. The players swim as far as they can under water using their arms and legs. When the race is finished, have each player sit on the deck at the point where they stopped.

Variation: The game is more challenging if the leader has the players swim using legs only, arms only, or no arms or no legs. The leader can be very creative with the options.

Ducks and Sharks

How to Play: Divide the players into two teams. Each team moves to opposite sides of the pool. One team swims on top of the water. These players are the ducks. The team on the opposite side swims under water. These players are the sharks.

On signal, both teams swim toward the opposite end of the pool at the same time. The first player from each team that makes it to the other end of the pool by swimming on top and under water wins. Switch the ducks and sharks after each round.

Watermelon Race

Props: Whole watermelons; a stopwatch

How to Play: Players line up on one side of the pool. Depending on how many watermelons are available, the leader can choose whether the players compete against each other or whether to time each player's race.

Players jump in the pool, and each receives a watermelon. Watermelons float well in the pool. The players must swim down to the finish line while pushing their watermelons. The players cannot lift the watermelons out of the water.

33

Torpedo Ready

How to Play: The object of this game is to see which player can go the far-thest. Designate an adult or a strong person to be the torpedo launcher. Each player will be a torpedo.

When it is time to launch, have a player float face down with hands stretched out in front. The launcher will say, "Torpedo ready!" at which point the launcher will push the torpedo by the feet to launch her.

Someone on the deck will mark how far the torpedo traveled. The torpedo who travels the farthest wins.

Variation: Divide the players into two teams, and designate one player on each team to be the launcher. Each team launches a torpedo at the same time, and the team whose torpedo goes farther gets a point. The first team to get to a predetermined score wins the game.

Categories

How to Play: Designate one player to be the leader. The leader stays touching his side of the pool while standing alone with his back toward the other players. All other players stand along the opposite side of the pool while touching their side.

The leader chooses one category and announces it to the group. The other players gather together and quietly tell each other which item in that category each of them will be. During this time, the leader ducks under water so he can't hear the other players' choices.

Once the players have chosen what they are going to be, the leader keeps his back to the group and calls out items from the category. When a player's item is called out, she quietly races to the leader's side of the pool. If the leader thinks he hears someone moving, he quickly turns around and races to the players' side of the pool. If the leader wins the race, he remains the leader. If he loses, the person who won the race becomes the new leader.

Examples

- Trees — fir, oak, birch...
- Cereals — Special K, cornflakes, Grape-Nuts...
- Cars — Chevrolet, VW, Nissan...
- Colors — blue, yellow, red...
- Dogs — poodles, dobermans, pit bulls...
- Candy bars — 100 Grand, Twix, Snickers...

Individual Games

Cannonball Contest

Props: Diving board; several sets of cards numbered from one to ten (both optional)

How to Play: Designate a panel of judges. The judges will stay on the side of the pool and will judge the size of the splash made from each cannonball.

Each player takes a turn performing a cannonball from the side of the pool or from a diving board. To make the cannonball, a player jumps as high as possible. As she does this, she bends her body, raising her knees to her chest and wrapping her arms around her knees. Her chin should be tucked.

Note: It is more fun if judges use cards as they do in the Olympics. The cards should be numbered from one to ten. The number one is for hardly any splash at all, and ten is for a tidal wave!

Underwater Bowling

How to Play: The object of this game is to touch as many bowling pins as possible. The twist is that the bowling ball and the pins are players, and all of this is played under water.

Designate one person to be the bowling ball, and the other players to be the pins. The pins go under water a good distance from the "ball." They must stay close together and remain in a tucked position, trying not to move. The ball goes under water and pushes off of the wall, with arms outstretched, in the direction of the "pins." The ball tries to tag as many pins as he can. Although the ball can move his arms to tag the pins, he cannot swim; he must only use the momentum from the push.

The leader records the number of pins tagged. Next, another player takes a turn as the ball. The ball who tags the most pins is the winner.

Variations:

1. The "ball" keeps her eyes closed.
2. The game is played across the width of the pool. There are two lanes, each with two (rotating) balls. As pins are tagged, they leave the water. Score the game the same way you do a bowling game.

Individual Games

Name the Jump

How to Play: This is a funny game to watch. One player is the caller and stays on the deck of the pool. The rest of the players line up on the deck of the pool. Each player takes a turn jumping into the air. Once the jumper is in the air, the caller yells the type of jump the player must perform.

Examples

- Cannonball
- Pencil
- Running
- Turn around

Variation: This game can be played using a diving board.

La-La-La— Ahhhhh!

Props: Garden hose

How to Play: This game is similar to musical chairs and always makes people laugh! An adult or older child assumes responsibility for turning on and off the garden hose. The person in charge of turning the water on and off must have her back toward the players, so nobody will know who will get sprayed!

Players sit in a line on the edge of the pool. The leader shouts, "Go!" Then, players must pass the hose from player to player. Young players should point the hose toward their stomachs. Teenagers can point the hose toward their faces. The adult randomly turns the hose on and off. The player who gets a face or stomach full of water is eliminated from the game and has to jump into the pool; the winner is the last player left.

Individual Games

Pickle

Props: Beach ball, or for an underwater game, use a toypedo

How to Play: Designate two players to be throwers. All other players must be in the middle of the pool. The middle of the pool is the "pickle." The object of this game is to have the players in the middle catch the object. Then the person who last threw the object gets stuck in the pickle. The player who caught the object becomes a thrower.

Variation: This game can be played under water with a toypedo. The throwers can be at opposite ends of the pool. They then launch the toypedo toward the middle of the pool. If someone catches the toypedo, the thrower gets stuck in the pickle.

Individual Games

That's My Number!

How to Play: Designate one player to be the caller. The other players stand on the side of the pool. Give every player on the side of the pool a number.

Next, the caller yells two numbers. The players with those numbers jump in the pool and quickly swim to the other side for safety. The caller jumps in after the players and tries to capture them. Any players who the caller tags are imprisoned on the sidelines until the game is over. The game ends or a new caller is picked and a new game is started when all of the players are tagged or at a predetermined time set by the leader.

Long Jump

Props: Noodle

How to Play: This game requires an adult to be the judge and to be in the water. The judge holds the noodle about one foot away from the diving board or the side of the pool.

Next, the players line up and take turns jumping over the noodle. When every player has jumped over the noodle, the judge moves the noodle further away from the diving board or side of the pool. If a player touches the noodle, or doesn't make it over the noodle, he is out. The winner is the player who jumps the farthest.

Individual Games

Below the Surface

Props: Beach ball

How to Play: Players stand in a circle in water that reaches their belly buttons. One player passes a beach ball under water to the next player. The next player grabs the beach ball without letting it surface and passes it on.

The object of the game is for the players to pass the beach ball without the beach ball popping to the surface. A player who lets the ball pop up to the surface is eliminated from the game. The player left standing is the winner. If you have many players, set a time limit to this game.

Variation: To make this game more challenging for advanced players, coat the beach ball with petroleum jelly!

Aqua Golf

Props: Golf club; whiffle ball; raft

How to Play: On the deck of the pool set up a towel, whiffle ball, and golf club. Put a raft in the pool. Each player takes a turn using a golf club to putt the ball onto the raft.

Variation: For older children, have one person in the pool create waves to make this game more challenging.

Weightless Challenge

Props: The leader can select the props—be creative!

How to Play: The leader creates a list of tasks depending on the props being used. The leader reads a number of tasks to the players. Then, the players go under water and perform the tasks. The object of the game is to complete as many tasks under water as possible before surfacing for air.

Examples

- Tie a shoe
- Sit cross-legged on the bottom of the pool for two seconds
- Do a handstand
- Pick up coins
- Jump rope
- Swim through a hula hoop

Individual Games

Piñaqua

Props: Trash bag filled with toys that float; a plastic bat; pole (optional)

How to Play: Fill a trash bag with a tiny bit of water and some toys that float. Tie this piñata to the end of a pole or hold the bag. Dangle the piñata over the pool. The players take turns trying to hit the bag with the plastic bat as they are jumping into the pool. Only one child jumps in the pool at a time; the others sit along the side of the pool. Keep the other children at a safe distance from the swinging plastic bat.

Sink the Sub

Props: At least one toypedo; diving/snorkeling mask or goggles

How to Play: This game is a variation of dodge ball. The leader should discuss appropriate ways to tag with the toypedo. For example, hitting another player in the face with the toypedo is inappropriate. Also, set a time limit on each round so that everyone has a turn. In this game, one player tries to tag the other player with a toypedo. Designate one player to be the captain and the other player to be the submarine, and make sure the players stay at least ten feet apart from each other during the course of the game. Give the captain the toypedo. The submarine should wear a diving mask or goggles.

Both players go under water. The captain tries to tag the submarine with the toypedo. The submarine swims around dodging the incoming toypedo. Once the toypedo has either hit or missed the submarine, the players switch roles.

Underwater Leader

How to Play: This game builds confidence and teaches young swimmers to keep their eyes open under water. The leader should have the players form a line with their backs against the side of the pool. The leader, who is also in the pool, asks the first player to step away from the wall and come to where the leader is standing. The leader and the player go under water, and the leader shows the "secret movement." The movement should be as creative as possible. Then this player will ask the next player to swim to him, and he will show her the "secret movement" under water so she can show it to the next player and so on. Continue this game until the movement comes back to the leader.

Examples

- Pinching a nose
- Yawning
- Nodding a head
- Tickling toes

even number

2 or more

Individual Games

Push 'Em Back

Props: Noodles

How to Play: This game tests the strength of one swimmer against another. The object is for one player to push away her opponent, using the noodles. For safety and to ensure players have fun, match two players who are similar in strength.

First, designate a referee; this person stands on the deck of the pool to decide which player wins. Each player floats on his front side, with arms stretched out in front of his head, holding a noodle. Position both players so that their noodles are touching.

On the referee's signal, the players begin kicking their legs as hard as they can to try to push back their opponent with their noodles. The referee will let the players know before the game starts how far back one player must push their opponent to win.

Message in the Bottle

Props: Empty two-liter bottles; "tasks" written on paper

How to Play: Write "tasks" on small pieces of paper and insert them into several two-liter plastic bottles. Tasks can be creative, silly, or difficult for the players. Adjust the tasks depending on the age and skill level of the players. Put one task in each bottle. Make sure it can be read through the bottle. Tightly seal the caps, and throw the bottles into the pool.

Each player jumps in and retrieves one bottle. She opens the cap, takes out the paper, reads it, and performs the task. If it is too hard to pull out the paper, the player can read the task through the bottle without opening the cap.

Examples

- Do twenty-five jumping jacks in the pool.
- Quack like a duck.
- Do a somersault in the pool.
- Do a handstand in the pool.

Variation: This game can also be used to begin a treasure hunt. The bottle could hold the map to the treasure.

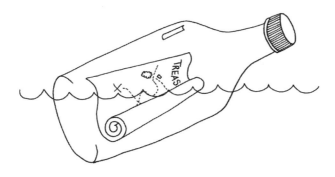

Individual Games

The Toilet Flush

How to Play: Players stand in a circle inside the pool. On a signal, everyone runs in the same direction as fast as they can. They do this within their circle to create a whirlpool. Then, on a signal, everyone lifts their feet off the bottom of the pool and assumes a tucked position. The whirlpool carries everyone around in a circle. As the whirlpool slows down, it is difficult to stay in the tucked position.

The object of the game is to be the last player floating in a tucked position. Once a player leaves the tucked position, they are eliminated from the game. The player (or players) remaining wins.

Team Games

Team games work best with large groups. To make this type of game successful, players must work together. Team games stress the importance of taking turns, cooperation, and performing a designated role or task for the good of the group.

Problem-solving games require the participation and ideas of all members. Children will develop social skills by learning how to express their ideas and giving input to team strategy.

To avoid hurt feelings, don't let the players pick teams. The leader must fairly divide the teams. Try to have a balance of players of varying abilities so that both teams will have similar overall skill levels.

even number | 6 or more

Team Games

Steal the Bacon

Props: Ball, empty two-liter plastic bottle with cap on it, or another imaginative prop that will be the "bacon"

This game is a classic. It is fun for everyone!

How to Play: Divide players into two teams. Teams line up in the water along the edge of the pool. Team members count off simultaneously so that each player on one team is matched with a player with the same number on the other team.

The leader throws the "bacon" into the center of the pool between the two teams and calls out a number. The two players who have that number swim to retrieve the bacon. The player who takes the bacon may swim to either team line in order to score a point. Once one player takes the bacon, the other player may tag him. If a player is tagged before getting to the line, no point is scored.

Variation: To make the game a little more challenging, the leader may call out two numbers.

Water-Balloon Volleyball

Props: A net or rope; water balloons

How to Play: This game follows standard volleyball rules and is fun when played either in or out of the pool. Designate a time limit. Divide the players into two teams. Set the net or rope in the middle of the pool. The players then begin tossing the water balloons back and forth.

The object of this game is to play volleyball in the water with water balloons. The winning team is the one that has the least amount of balloons broken on their side. Be sure to clean up the pieces of balloon when the game is finished.

Team Games

To Catch a Thief

Props: An item that floats

How to Play: One player stands guard over an item that floats. Everyone else is a thief that tries to steal the floating item. If the guard tags a thief, that player must freeze and stay floating in his or her spot for the rest of the game.

The guard cannot hold the treasure; it must be floating within its space. The guard may leave the treasure to catch a thief, but then another thief can steal the item. Whoever steals the treasure is the guard for the next game. Be sure to set a time limit for each game.

Team Games

Baseball

Props: Plastic bat or noodle; sponge ball

How to Play: Everybody loves to play baseball. Played in the water, it is even more fun.

Divide the players into two teams. Determine where the bases will be located around the pool. Place one team in the outfield and the other at bat.

Consider setting a limit on the number of swings each team can have to keep it a fast-moving game. You can also use only one out and switch the teams.

Variation: Make this game more challenging by having the batter swim to the bases, run backward, or jump to the bases.

Team Games

Body Tug of War

How to Play: The more the merrier with this game. It is a great game to play with adults. Explain to the players where the middle line is and how much they have to pull to win the game.

Divide the group into two even teams. Designate the strongest person to be the captain of each team. The rest of the players form the links in a chain. They float on top of the water (face up or face down), holding on to the ankles of the teammate in front of them. When both teams are assembled, the two players at the front of the lines join hands in order to form a chain comprised of both teams. The captains stand at the end of their chains.

On the signal, the captains hold the ankles of the last players in their team's chains and pull, in an effort to pull the agreed-upon portion of the other team's chain over the middle line. The captains can wiggle the chain of bodies back and forth in order to create movement. If the chain breaks, reassemble and try again.

Team Games

Seahorse Toss

Props: Noodles and plastic or foam rings

How to Play: Divide the group into pairs. One partner will sit on the noodle, and the other will stand outside the pool on the deck.

   The player on the side of the pool tosses one ring at a time onto the longer end of the noodle, which represents the neck of a "seahorse." The partner on the seahorse may assist in directing the neck of the seahorse to capture the ring. The pair with the most rings around their noodle at the end of the game wins.

Note: You may choose to have the player on the side of the pool toss the rings to the part of the noodle that is sticking out behind the player in the water.

Team Games

Dirty Backyard Cleanup

Props: Balls; balloons; sponges…

This is a fun game in and out of the pool.

How to Play: Lay a rope or garden hose across the pool in order to divide the pool in half. Group the players into two teams. Each team assumes a position on one side of the line, and the area on their side of the line becomes their team's "backyard." The leader tosses balloons or other items that float in the pool between the two teams. When the leader says, "Go!" the players have two minutes to toss the items over the line into the other team's backyard. When the time is up, the team with the cleanest backyard wins!

58

Team Games

Underwater Rugby

Props: Ball; goggles; and maybe a goal at each end

How to Play: Divide the players into two teams. Designate each team's goal. Instruct the players that they must not hold on to any player or a penalty will be issued.

Each player holds on to the wall of the pool. The leader throws the ball into the middle, and the teams race to get it. Players try to get the ball in the opponent's goal, but the players can only move the ball while swimming under water. If a player needs to come up for a breath, she must pass the ball under water to another teammate. A player cannot come to the surface with the ball or a penalty will be issued. A penalty can be giving the ball to the opposite team. The team that gets the most goals is the winner.

Octopus Race

How to Play: Divide the players into two or more teams. Choose the strongest swimmers to be the leads. Each swimmer floats on his stomach or back. He must use one hand to hold on to the ankle of his teammate's foot in front of him. In this way, the players form their team's "octopus." They use their free hand to help the "octopus" travel.

On the word, "Go!" each team races toward the designated finish line. If the team becomes separated, they must reattach themselves and continue.

Team Games

Ping-Pong Scramble

Props: Ping-pong balls or balloons; buckets

How to Play: Divide the players into teams. Designate a bucket as the goal for each team.

All players hold on to the wall. Toss all the balls or balloons into the pool. Players collect one ball at a time, swim back to their bucket or goal, and place the ball in the bucket. Then, they swim back to retrieve another ball. They can bring only one ball at a time. The team that collects the most balls is the winner.

Variation: The children can play this game individually as well, in which case each child should have her own bucket or goal.

Team Games

Scavenger Hunt

Props: Many items to be placed at the bottom of the pool

How to Play: Divide the players into teams. Give each team a list of all of the things they must collect from the bottom of the pool. On the word, "Go!" they must swim around and collect only the items on their list. The team to collect all of their items first is the winner.

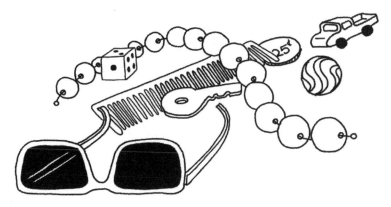

Examples

- Coins
- Pieces of clothing
- Rocks
- Toys

Team Games

Obstacle Course

Props: Hula hoops; rafts; noodles

How to Play: I love obstacle courses. The more creative you are, the more successful the obstacle course will be. Set up two identical obstacle courses in and/or around the pool. Leave enough room between the obstacles for children to navigate safely. Vary the number and the difficulty of the obstacles based on the ages and the skill levels of the players. If the pool is not large enough for two courses, the leader may use a stopwatch and time each team.

Divide the players into two teams. Each player takes a turn navigating the obstacle course. The next player in the team can start the course only when the one before him is finished with it. The team in which all the players finish the obstacle course first—or in the least time—is the winner.

Examples of obstacles and activities

- Hula hoop to dive through, jump through, or up and through
- Noodles or rafts to ride
- Items to collect from the bottom of the pool
- Beach balls to throw into a bucket
- Swimming under water
- Tossing a ring on a noodle
- Performing a cannonball

Variation: The leader can have children play this game individually as well. Then, each player should be timed as she travels through the obstacle course. A player can go multiple times with the goal being to improve upon her own best time.

63

Team Games

Dodge the Sponge

Props: Big sponges

How to Play: This game is a variation of classic dodge ball. Only here, players are dodging the sponge!

Divide the players into two teams. Separate the teams on either side of the pool. Show them where the middle of the pool is and let them know they cannot cross this line. Give an equal number of sponges to both sides.

At a signal, the players try to hit the opposing players with the sponges. Any player that is hit is eliminated from the game. If a player from the opposing team catches the sponge, the player who threw the sponge is out. The team with the greatest number of players left is the winner.

Team Games

Sponge Toss

Props: Really wet sponges, the bigger the better

How to Play: Divide the players into pairs. Give each pair one really wet sponge. Partners stand close to one another. On the word, "Go!" one player throws the wet sponge, and their partner tries to catch it. After each successful catch, players take one step backward. The game continues until there is only one team left. That team is the winner.

65

Team Games

Backseat Driver

Props: Items that float, such as corks, balloons, or ping-pong balls; rafts

How to Play: Divide the players into teams. Decide how many teams will play at one time based upon how many rafts are available. Assign at least two players per raft (per team). The person on the front of the raft closes his eyes. He is the person driving the car. The backseat driver gives verbal directions to the driver. She cannot help the driver steer the car. Before the game starts, the game leader decides whether the driver or the backseat driver must pick up the objects.

The object of the game is to have the backseat driver be as descriptive as possible so that the driver can maneuver the car around the pool to pick up the floating objects. The team that collects all of the objects in the shortest period of time wins.

Keep It Up

Props: Water balloons or sponges

How to Play: Divide the players into two or more teams. Each team forms a line.

The first person in line throws the balloon or sponge high in the sky and then runs or swims to the back of the line while the next person in line tries to catch the balloon. This continues until everyone on the team has had a chance to catch the balloon. If a player does not catch the balloon, the throw must be repeated. The team that finishes first wins.

Team Games

Take out the Garbage!

How to Play: Divide the players into two teams. Designate two team captains, or "collectors." The other players assume the role of "garbage" and line up against one side of the pool; the collectors go to the opposite side of the pool.

At the leader's signal, the collectors run or swim to the opposite side to collect their "garbage." They can take only 2 "bags" at a time. The players, or garbage bags, must hook their arms around the arms of the collector and keep their feet off of the ground at all times. Then, the collector takes the garbage bags to the other side of the pool, drops them off, and then returns for more garbage. The collector who finishes collecting all of the garbage bags first is the winner.

Team Games

Basketball Bomb

Props: Water balloons; two hula hoops

How to Play: Use one balloon in the game, but have several ready in case one pops. Set up a hula hoop at each end of the pool. The hoops will float around; this makes the game more interesting.

Divide the players into two teams. Each team tries to score points by shooting the balloon into their opponent's hoop. The first team to reach ten baskets wins.

Attack or Retreat

Props: Coin

How to Play: Divide the players into two teams. Designate the strongest swimmers on each team the captains. Both teams face each other in the center of the pool; one team is heads and the other is tails. The leader flips the coin on the deck of the pool. The captains must be close enough to the coin toss to see it. Depending on which side of the coin wins, the captains tell their troops to attack or retreat.

The attacking team tries to capture the opposing team's members by tagging them. If a player is tagged, he is now on the team that tagged him, but if the opposing players make it back to the wall, they are safe and remain on the same team. The game ends either when one team has captured everyone from the opposing team or when the leader decides the game should end. If not everyone has been captured, the team with more players wins.

Team Games

Basketball H2O

Props: A noodle for each player; beach ball; two goals made from objects, such as laundry baskets or boxes

How to Play: This game can be played just like basketball; the only difference is the players are riding noodles in the water. Divide the players into two teams. Designate a referee; this person stays outside of the pool to monitor the game, keep score, toss the ball in the center to begin the game, and chase after any stray balls. Depending on the skill and age level of the players, the leader decides on the rules of the game. It can be as easy as all team members trying to score points or structured with designated positions. The team that scores the most points wins.

Note: A time limit is recommended with this game.

Team Games

Diving-Board Baseball

Props: Ball; plastic bat or noodle; bases

How to Play: Divide the players into two teams. Place one team in the field and one team at bat. Designate a leader, preferably an adult, to be the pitcher and referee for both teams. The leader may follow the rules of baseball or modify the rules to suit the number of players or skill level of the group. The game continues until three outs, and then the teams switch positions.

Examples

- The batter will come to the edge of the diving board or pool and try to hit the ball. If the batter swings and misses, she is out.
- If the player hits the ball, the ball must land in the pool.
- There are no home runs. After a hit, the batter will jump into the water and swim to first base, or as many bases as possible, without getting tagged. If the batter safely makes it to one base, the next teammate is up to bat.
- The base runner may steal a base by swimming under water.

Out-of-the-Pool Games

If you feel the kids need a rest from the pool games, or if some kids are eliminated from a game, these out-of-pool games will keep them happily occupied. Each game involves water, so bathing suits and water shoes are needed.

Be sure to have a talk about safety before beginning any of the games. Water might make the area around the pool slippery. Caution children to be careful when walking or running.

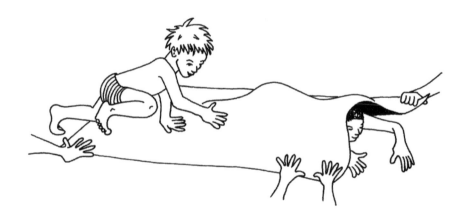

Hole in My Bucket!

Props: Cups with holes; two buckets for each team or each player. A wet sponge can be substituted for the cup with holes.

How to Play: Decide where the goals and the starting line will be. Then, set up an empty bucket at each goal. Place another bucket full of water at the starting line. Divide the players into teams. At the starting line, give each player a cup with holes.

On the leader's signal, each player fills her cup with water and places the cup on her head; players can hold the cup with their hands to prevent it from falling. They run or walk to their goal and empty the cups into the buckets. Next, they run back to the water bucket, fill their cups again, and repeat.

The leader decides how long to play the game. The winner is the player with the most water in his bucket.

Quick Draw

Props: Paint brushes; spray bottles; sponges; rubber stamps; watercolor paints; food coloring; a concrete or cement surface (or some paper)

How to Play: This is a fun game for kids of all ages when they need a break from the water.

Gather different spray bottles and pails. Fill them with water. Add a different food coloring to each container of water. Gather an assortment of different tools, such as paint brushes and rubber stamps. Be creative with the tools.

Then, each artist draws a picture on the cement or a sheet of paper as quickly as possible before it dries. If no coloring is used, the drawing will rapidly disappear before the players eyes!

Note: As a safety precaution, make sure the cement is not too hot before beginning this game.

Out-of-the-Pool Games

Splash

Props: Water balloons

How to Play: Assign a number to each player and choose one player to be a caller. The players stand in a circle while the caller stands in the center with a water balloon.

The caller shouts a number and throws the water balloon high in the air. The player with that number runs to the center to catch the water balloon. While the player catches the water balloon, all the other players scatter, but when the balloon is caught, the catcher yells, "Freeze!" All players must freeze.

Then, the catcher seeks an easy target and throws the water balloon at that player. The player may duck or swerve to avoid getting hit. If the player is hit, or if the catcher fails to catch the balloon, then that person is the next caller.

Cat and Mouse

Props: Large bedsheet or tablecloth

How to Play: Designate one player to be the cat and one to be the mouse. All other players kneel down on the ground holding onto the edge of the sheet.

The cat needs to find and tag the mouse. The mouse crawls around under the sheet, and the cat crawls around on top of the sheet. The rest of the players shake the sheet up and down or side-to-side, puffing the sheet up so that the cat has difficulty seeing and finding the mouse.

If the cat tags the mouse, the game is over. Then, the leader chooses other players to be the cat and the mouse.

Out-of-the-Pool Games

Shark Attack!

Props: Large bedsheet or tablecloth

How to Play: Designate one person to be the lifeguard and one to be the shark. Everyone else will be a player. The shark goes under the sheet. Everyone else sits on the ground holding onto the sheet with his or her feet hidden under the sheet.

Next, have the players quickly shake the sheet up and down, but not too high. It's best to keep the element of surprise! As the players move the sheet, the shark crawls around on her hands and knees and selects her victim. The shark grabs the feet of an innocent victim and tries to pull the victim under the sheet. The victim screams for help to the lifeguard.

The lifeguard runs to the rescue and tries to pull the victim out before the victim is pulled under the sheet. If the victim is pulled under the sheet, he also becomes a shark.

Notes:

- The sharks usually win because by the time a few kids are pulled under the sheet, the number of sharks is so high that it is impossible for one lifeguard to rescue all of the victims at once.
- I recommend setting a time limit on this game.

Out-of-the-Pool Games

Pop-up

Props: Water balloons; tablecloth or bedsheet

How to Play: This is a really quick game. Players stand around the sheet. Then, the leader places all of the water balloons on the sheet. On a signal, the players grab the sheet and pull it, throwing the water balloons up in the air.

Next, players let go of the sheet. They try to catch a water balloon before it hits the ground.

Variation: Instead of filling the balloons with water, fill them with small candy or blow them up, and let the kids catch the balloons!

78

Out-of-the-Pool Games

Blindfolded Guards

Props: Two chairs; wet sponges or squirt guns

How to Play: Designate two players to be the guards. Guards sit in chairs facing each other. Leave enough room between the chairs so that two other players can sneak between them. Blindfold the guards and hand them either a wet sponge or squirt guns or bottles. Assign each remaining player a partner.

The partners then try to quietly sneak through the two guards. If the guards think someone is passing through, they throw the sponge or use the squirt gun to attack the intruders. If an intruder is hit, that player becomes one of the blindfolded guards.

Note: This game can be played in the water too! It's a great game for parents to play; the funny part of this game is that the guards end up squirting each other most of the time. Kids love to see their parents be the guards!

Graveyard

How to Play: This is a great cool-down game to help the kids relax. Designate one person to be the graveyard keeper. Everyone else pretends to be dead. All of the dead must lie perfectly still with their eyes closed and no laughing or wiggling!

Next, the graveyard keeper begins walking around. She moves each player into funny positions to try to get them to laugh. If the dead laugh or wiggle, they are eliminated from the game.

Note: As a precaution, the leader should set ground rules and discuss appropriate positions and ways of touching before beginning this game.

Out-of-the-Pool Games

Pass the Sponge

Props: Sponge; bucket of water

How to Play: Divide the players into teams. Each team forms a line. Designate a bucket and a sponge for each team.

On a signal, the first team member grabs the sponge from the bucket and passes it overhead to the person behind him. That person then passes the sponge through their legs to the person behind them, and the players that follow continue alternating between passing the sponge through their legs and overhead. When the sponge reaches the end of the line, the last player returns the sponge by passing it to the person in front of her in a way that is different from how she received it (i.e., if she received it overhead, she returns it through her legs). The first team to finish is the winner!

Note: This game can be played in the water too!

Out-of-the-Pool Games

Wash 'n' Run

Props: Wet clothes (the leader decides which type of clothes to use...shirt, pants, socks, hat, gloves); big bucket

How to Play: Place the clothes in a big bucket filled with water. Choose a starting line and a finish line. Divide the players into teams. Team sizes will depend on the number of available pieces of clothing.

Players line up at the starting line. On the leader's signal, one player from each team runs to the bucket filled with wet clothes and tries to put on one piece of clothing as quickly as possible. Then, the player runs back to the finish line. The next player takes a turn and so on. The team that finishes first is the winner.

Variation: This game can be played individually as well. Put similar sets of clothing (i.e., one shirt, one sock, and one hat) in separate buckets for each player. The player who puts on all the clothes and runs back to the finish line first is the winner.

Note: This game can be played in the water too!

Garden-Hose Limbo

Props: Garden hose

How to Play: If it is a hot day, this is a fun way to cool down. An adult or older player holds the garden hose. Players form a line and begin to "limbo" under the water from the hose. Each time the round is finished, lower the garden hose until players have to crawl under the water. There doesn't have to be a winner with this one, it's just fun.

Racing Games

Racing games can be strenuous and can quickly raise a player's heart rate. This category of games is useful for developing endurance, muscle strength, and conditioning.

Racing games require more than one player. Yet since there is little to no preparation for each game, they can be inserted into a schedule anytime.

Be sure to know the skill level of each child to choose the appropriate racing game. If there is a group of children with various swimming abilities, divide the groups into fair teams.

even number

4 or more

Racing Games

Jump Shot

Props: Beach ball

How to Play: The object of this game is to successfully toss a beach ball back and forth with a partner.

Decide on a starting line and a finish line. Divide the players into pairs. One player from each pair stands on the deck at the opposite end of the pool. Their partner is in the pool at the starting line.

At the leader's signal, the partner on the deck tosses the ball to the player in the water. The player in the water must jump to catch the ball and immediately tosses the ball back to her partner. If the toss is successful, the player in the water may advance one step and continue the game. The first pair to reach the finish line wins.

Racing Games

Cruise Ship

Props: Little plastic figures, such as army men

How to Play: Decide on the location of a starting line and a finish line. Divide the players into teams. Give each team the same number of plastic toys. The plastic toys are the "passengers." The object of this game is to carry the most passengers as fast as possible from the starting line to the finish line.

Each team designates one player to be the captain; the other players are cruise ships. The cruise ships float on their backs or stomachs. To begin play, each captain places passengers (plastic toys) on the backs or stomachs of the cruise ships where they have the least chance of falling off.

Each cruise ship must now carry the figures all the way to the finish line. The team that gets the most passengers to the finish line wins.

Variation: If there are no plastic figures, the game can be played as "Cargo Ship." Then, players transport other objects, such as balls, pennies, and so on.

85

 even number

 4 or more

Racing Games

Sponge Relay

Props: Wet sponges

How to Play: Divide the players into two groups. Have each group line up on opposite sides of the pool, facing the other players, and assign players to two teams (A and B) as follows: On one side start by assigning players to team "A," so the line goes A, B, A, B, and so on. On the other side, start by assigning the first player to team "B" (i.e., B, A, B, A, etc.), so teammates do not end up facing each other but instead are situated diagonally across the pool from one another. Give a sponge to the first team member on either side. Be sure these sponges are soaking wet.

On the leader's signal, the team members throw the sponge to their team member who is on a diagonal from them. Every time a player drops the sponge, it becomes more soaked. Players are not allowed to wring the sponge. It must stay heavy and wet. The players continue to pass the sponge down the line and back again. The first team to complete this task wins.

Racing Games

Crossing the River

Props: Two ropes the length of the pool; two rafts

How to Play: To prepare for this game, string two ropes the length of the pool. Be sure to tie the ropes to something secure. If there isn't a place to tie the ropes, team members on each side of the pool can hold the ropes.

Divide the players into two teams. Then divide each team in half. Place one half of the team at one end of the pool and the remaining half at the other end of the pool.

On the leader's signal, the first player in line from each team will carefully climb onto the raft, from the deck of the pool or in the water. Using the rope, they will pull the raft to the other side and climb off. The next team member will do the same. The game continues until all players have participated. The first team to finish or the driest team wins.

Seahorses and Mermaids

How to Play: Designate one person to be the caller. Divide the rest of the players into pairs. One member of each pair will be the seahorse, while the partner becomes the mermaid. The seahorses stand in a circle formation in the water, and the mermaids stand behind the seahorses.

To begin play, the caller shouts either "mermaids" or "seahorses." If the caller says "mermaids," the mermaids must swim like a mermaid with their legs together clockwise around the circle. They then resume their place behind their partner, the seahorse. The last mermaid to reach his place is eliminated and so is the partner.

When the caller says, "seahorses," the seahorses must back out and swim under water between the mermaids' legs. They then swim clockwise around the circle until they reach their partner again. Then, they swim between their partner's legs and back into the starting position. The last seahorse in place is eliminated and so is the partner. The last mermaid and seahorse remaining are the winners.

Note: As a safety precaution, less-skilled swimmers should play this game in the shallow end of the pool.

88

Chase the Ball

Props: Beach ball

How to Play: In this game, the players must move the ball to the other end of the pool. What makes this game so hard is that they cannot touch the ball with their hands. Instead, they may kick it or pop it with their head or nose.

Racing Games

89

Popcorn Races

Props: One beach ball or balloon per person

How to Play: Players line up at the starting line. The object of this game is for a player to keep a beach ball between his legs as he jumps up and down to the finish line.

Give each player a beach ball to put between his legs. On the signal, each player jumps up and down to the finish line. If someone loses the ball, they must retrieve it and continue to jump. The first player to the finish line wins.

Note: If there are a lot of players, this game can be played as a relay race.

Hold My Baby, Please!

Props: Pacifier; diaper; baby bonnet...

How to Play: Designate a starting line and a finish line. Then, divide the players into teams. Ask one player on each team to be the "baby." Since everyone becomes almost weightless in the water, the baby doesn't have to be the lightest person. Tell the babies that they can kick, scream, cry, suck their thumbs, and so on.

The object of the game is for a team to work together to carry their baby to the finish line. The team that gets their baby to the finish line first is the winner!

Variation: If there is a large group of players, they can pass the baby to the next team player in line. The first team to pass their baby to the last person in line is the winner.

Racing Games

NASCAR
Races

Props: Rafts

How to Play: Divide the players into teams. Designate a starting line and a finish line. Be sure you have enough rafts for each team. The leader decides the number of players on each raft. Sometimes the more players on a raft, the funnier the game is!

The players can sit on the raft, lie down on the raft, or ride backward on the raft. Be creative in the instructions given! On the leader's signal, the team propels their craft forward. The first team to get their raft to the finish line wins.

even
number

4 or
more

Racing Games

Over and Under

Props: A ball or balloon for each team, or anything to pass, such as something silly like a toy frog or duck

How to Play: Divide the players into teams. Each team forms a line. Give an object to the first person in line for each team. Players then pass the object overhead to the next player behind them in line. When the object reaches the last player, the method of passing the object changes. On the way back, the object must be passed between the legs. The first team that finishes the task is the winner.

Note: For beginners, this game should be played in shallow water. More advanced swimmers can play this game in deep water.

Racing Games

Stinky Feet

Props: Beach ball

How to Play: Divide the players into teams. Each team forms a line from one end of the pool to the other. Players float on their backs.

On the leader's signal, the first team member passes a beach ball to the next player. The ball can't be passed with hands—only the feet can be used! The team that completes this race first is the winner.

Racing Games

Tunnel Race

How to Play: Divide the players into teams. Choose one member from each team to swim in the tunnel. Have these members hold onto the side of the pool until ready. The rest of the team forms a line with their legs separated; this forms the tunnel.

On the word, "Go!" the tunnel swimmer quickly swims through the legs of her team to get to the other side of the tunnel. The game can end here, or it can continue by having that member join the tunnel team. Then, the next person in line is the tunnel swimmer.

Racing Games

Wet T-Shirt Race

Props: T-shirts (be sure all shirts are the same size and large enough to accommodate people of all shapes and sizes)

How to Play: This game provides a lot of laughs. Divide the players into teams. Teams form a line on the deck of the pool.

To begin play, the first member of each team must put on a wet T-shirt and jump in the water. They swim down to one end of the pool and back, take off the T-shirt in the water, and throw it to the next team member who is standing on the deck. The game continues in this manner until all players have had a turn. The winning team is the one that finishes first.

Racing Games

You've Got a Delivery

Props: Beach ball

How to Play: Divide the players into two teams. Designate one person from each team to go first. This person gets in the pool. Divide the rest of the teams in half. Half of each team's players go to opposite ends of the pool.

On the leader's signal, teammates toss the beach balls to their player in the pool. The player grabs the ball between her feet. Then, the player swims on her back to the end of the pool. She must toss or bring the ball up and out of the pool. Then, the next player from the team jumps into the pool, and a teammate tosses him the ball and so on. The game continues until one team wins.

Racing Games

Best Friends

How to Play: Designate the starting line and the finish line. Divide the group into pairs. The object of the game is for two players to swim as one, so try to pair individuals with similar swimming skills.

In each pair, one partner does the arm movements while the other holds onto their partner's ankles and does the leg movements. The pair who swims to the finish line first wins.

Racing Games

Back Me Up

How to Play: Divide the group into pairs. Place all pairs at the starting end of the pool. Pairs stand back-to-back while interlocking arms. Each partner faces a different side of the pool. The player who is facing the opposite end of the pool lifts his feet off the bottom of the pool. Meanwhile, his partner can keep her feet on the ground. She travels backward toward the opposite end of the pool while carrying her partner.

On the leader's signal, the pairs race to one end of the pool and tag the deck. Without turning around, they must switch roles. The player who was walking now takes her feet off the ground while her partner puts his feet on the ground and travels backward to the finish line. The pair who makes it to the finish line first wins.

Swimming Races

How to Play: Designate a starting line and a finish line. Depending on the skill level of the players, this game can be played with one lap across a swimming pool or many laps back and forth to the finish line. The leader can designate the kind of swimming strokes that must be used. Before the races begin, be sure each player knows the different styles of swimming strokes they should use: forward crawl, backstroke, breaststroke, sidestroke, doggie paddle, or freestyle.

Players line up on the deck of the pool. The leader signals and shouts a swimming stroke. On the signal, the players jump into the pool and race to the other side, using the designated swimming stroke. As noted above, adding additional laps can extend the race. Each lap can use a different swimming stroke.

Variation: With ten or more players, this game can become a tag team game. In this style of play, one teammate tags the hand of the next player in line. Then that player continues the race.

Note: For an additional challenge, or if one player has an unfair advantage over the other players, have the advanced swimmer place a small ball, kickboard, or some object that floats between his ankles to prevent him from using his legs during the race.

The Kentucky Derby

How to Play: This game can be done in pairs or in teams. If playing teams, assign a partner to each team member. One partner will be the "horse." The other player will be the "jockey." Or each jockey may ride a noodle.

To begin play, one member from each team gets into the pool. They get on the "horse's" back. On the word, "Go!" the jockeys and their horses race to the other end of the pool and back. The team that finishes first is the winner.

Pass and Shoot

Props: Beach ball; laundry basket; stopwatch

How to Play: The object of this game is for swimmers to pass a ball from swimmer to swimmer until one swimmer can shoot the ball into the basket.

Designate the starting line and finish line. Place the laundry basket at the finish line. Ask someone reliable to be the timer. This person will time each game and stand at the basket to catch stray balls. Divide the players into teams; the number of teams depends upon how wide or how many swimming lanes are in the pool. Players form a line in a swimming lane and one player is given the ball.

On the leader's signal, the players swim while continuously passing the ball from swimmer to swimmer until one player is close enough to shoot the ball into the basket. If the player misses, he may keep trying to shoot.

The team that completes this task in the least amount of time wins.

Water Exercises

This section of the book includes exercises that will increase the heart rate as well as stretch and tone muscles. Most of the exercises are written in a conversational style, so they can be simply read aloud to the children.

Exercise does not mean push-ups! Nearly any activity in which the body is in continuous movement for fifteen minutes or more can be a great benefit for a person's health, happiness, and self-esteem. To help our children burn fat and preserve lean muscle tissue, they should exercise every day. This is easier said than done, but when you bring a pool and kids together, there are many ways to have fun with fitness.

Kids shouldn't feel about exercise the same way they feel about homework. It shouldn't be something they feel they have to do. Exercise does not have to be structured, just adding an element of creativity and imagination can go a long way. The kids will be having so much fun that they won't even know they are doing something good for themselves.

Stretches

These stretches should be done in the pool before playing any of the games. Be sure to discuss general stretching guidelines with the children. Tell them not to bounce when stretching. They should not stretch to the point of saying, "Ouch." Urge children to relax as they stretch, and remind them to keep breathing. If they feel any discomfort, they should stop the stretch because pain is their body's way of saying that something is wrong.

Walking on Heels: Begin walking on the heels of your feet; this will help stretch the Achilles tendon behind your ankle and calf muscle.

Arm Circles: Stretch out arms wide at your side and begin circling your arms in one direction. Count to ten. Then reverse the circle and count to ten.

Cat Stretch: Have you ever seen how a cat stretches? It even feels good to watch them. In the shallow end of the pool, place your hands on your knees, arch your back, and count to ten. Be sure to keep your head down. Relax for a minute and try it again. Be sure your face doesn't go in the water!

Lateral Flex: Place your hands on top of your shoulder. Slowly bend to one side and hold, counting to ten. Then bend over to the other side and hold.

Heel to Bottom: Stand close to the wall of your pool. Hold on if you need to and bring your left heel toward your bottom. Hold the heel in place with your left hand and count to ten. Release and try this with your right leg.

Butterfly Wings: Sit on the deck of your pool with your knees pointing to each side and bring the bottom of your feet together. Hold your feet with your hands. Slowly raise your knees up and count to ten. Slowly lower your legs and count to ten. This is a good stretch for your inner thighs.

Smell Your Stinky Toes: Stay in the same position as mentioned above, but slowly bend over and try to smell your toes. You will feel this stretch in your lower back, buttocks, and hamstring (in the back of your thighs).

Hug Yourself: Wrap your arms around yourself and give yourself a big hug. This stretches your upper-back muscles.

Superman: In a standing position, place your hands on your hips and pull your shoulders back. You are now Superman, and you are stretching your chest and shoulder muscles.

Fold Yourself in Half: From a standing position, bend over and try to touch your toes. You will immediately feel this stretch in your hamstring muscle. Count to ten, roll back up to a standing position, and do it again.

Water Walking

Walking in the water is a great way to warm up the cardiovascular system. Begin with a slow walk, then gradually increase your speed. Try one of the fun variations below!

Walking Backward: Take little and big steps backward across your pool.

Sideways: Slowly take big steps sideways across your pool, then gradually make your steps larger until you are leaping sideways.

On Your Toes: Walk on your tiptoes.

Walk on Your Heels: Walk on your heels. Try this one immediately after you walk on your toes; it feels so good!

Tin Soldier: Walk stiff-legged across your pool like a tin soldier.

Cross-Over: Stand sideways and cross your right foot over your left foot. Walk this way continuously until you make it to the other side. Now repeat with your other leg.

Kick Backs: Instead of bringing your leg forward, kick back with a straight leg as you walk. Be careful not to arch your back.

Water Running

Running: Try one or all of these variations: run forward, backward, and sideways.

Running with High Knees: Imagine two tires at the bottom of your pool. Begin running; keep your shoulders back, and bring your knees up high.

Running and Stopping: Run full force eight steps ahead; stop and run backward eight steps; stop and repeat.

Gallop Around Your Pool: Gallop around your pool in a zigzag pattern or from corner to corner.

No Arms: Try running in chest-deep water with your arms tucked by your side.

Deep Water Running: Try running in the deep end of your pool. This is very challenging.

Run, Run, and Leap: In the shallow end of your pool, run three steps, and then leap into the air.

Jumping

Jumps can be done in deep or shallow water. For best results, try each jump ten times or more.

Assisted Jumps: Stand facing the wall of the pool. Place your hands on the deck to keep yourself upright. Using your legs, push up and off the bottom of the pool.

Long Jumps: Standing on one side of the pool, jump with both feet together as far forward as you can until you reach the other side. Repeat if you can!

Open Leg Jumps: While standing, jump and open your legs while pressing your arms out toward your legs at the same time.

Popcorn: Start at one end of your pool. Get into a tucked position and pop up and out of the water. Travel forward with each jump.

Tuck Jumps: Jump and bring your knees into your chest. Try to move across your pool and back.

Balance

Sit on a Beach Ball: This one takes some practice at first. But once you have it, it is a terrific exercise for your torso, too.

Stand on Your Noodle: This exercise is best done in the deep water. Step with both feet into the middle of the noodle. Hold this position as long as you can. For an additional challenge, try one leg at a time.

Close Your Eyes: Standing in chest-deep water, close your eyes and raise one leg from the bottom of the pool. Repeat with the other leg.

Swinging: In the deep end of your pool, sit on your noodle and try to swing.

Rafting: Lying face up on your raft, slowly raise one leg off the raft and hold. If this is easy, try lifting both legs at the same time.

Handstand: Try performing a handstand on the bottom of the pool. If this is easy, try performing a handstand with only one hand.

Push-Offs

I love push-offs, and children can have so much fun with these. They can even be made into a race. Try each one separately, and then add them all together.

Holding on to the edge of the pool, push off and float back as far as possible. Then move into an upright position, and run back to the wall. The following variations should be performed from the backfloat position (do not turn upright) unless otherwise specified. The variations can be performed separately or in combination (e.g., do a push-off, and from the backfloat position, do 2 alternate leg lifts followed by a run up the wall).

Alternate Leg Lifts: Slowly raise one leg, and then the other.

Frog Swim: Flip over and swim like a frog.

Jumping Jacks: Float on your back and do as many jumping jacks as you can.

Bicycle: While floating on your back, begin to move your legs in circles like you are riding a bicycle.

Tuck: Bring your legs into a tucked position, then extend them straight out again, and repeat.

Doggie Paddle: Flip over and swim like a dog.

Run up the Wall: Run as fast as you can up to the wall of the pool. With both feet, jump and push off of the wall as hard as you can. *Note:* This one is a little different, but kids love it.

Upper-Body Exercises

Baseball Practice: Practice swinging a baseball bat under water. This can also be done with an old golf club or tennis racquet. *Note:* Many professional athletes use this technique to strengthen their upper body.

Punching Arms: Hold an air-filled balloon under water and have each child try to punch the balloon as many times as she can. Be sure to hold the balloon away from your face.

Arm Curls: Standing in chest-deep water, bend your arms and cup your hands. Pull water toward the surface, then immediately flip your hands over and push the water behind your body. Repeat this ten times.

Swimming with Only Arms: These exercises are ideal for the intermediate or advanced swimmer. Starting at one end of the pool, have the swimmer place a small ball or kickboard between her ankles; this prevents her from using her legs. Choose from one of the following strokes. Remember to instruct swimmers to use only arms!

- Forward crawl
- Backstroke
- Breaststroke
- Sidestroke

Lower-Body Exercises

Cross-Country Skiing: Keep your body in an upright position, and extend your right leg a full step in front of your left foot. Bring your left arm in front of your body when your right foot is in front. Jump and switch your arm and leg positions. Travel around your pool.
Note: This exercise can be done in shallow or deep water.

Downhill Skiing: Jump side-to-side, keeping both legs together. Travel around your pool. To make this more challenging, jump with legs together three times, then on jump number four, spread your legs and arms to the side and repeat step one.

Speed Skating: Step on a diagonal with your right foot; let your left heel come toward your bottom while your arms swing together side to side. Repeat with your other side. Travel around your pool. *Note:* This exercise can be done in shallow or deep water.

Tick Tock: In a standing position, swing one leg as high as you can to your side, and immediately repeat with your other leg. You should feel like a clock pendulum.

Torso Strengthening

Torso Twist: Standing in chest-deep water, hold onto a foam disc or beach ball. Keeping both feet on the bottom of the pool, hold the ball under water with one hand on top and the other hand on the bottom. Pull in your stomach muscles and slowly twist your torso, dragging the disc from side to side.

Toe Touches: From a standing position, jump and bring both feet straight in front of your body. Try to touch your toes. Repeat this ten times.

Abdominal Crunches: Floating on your back, slowly bring your knees into your chest, and then return them to the starting position. Repeat this ten times.

Strong Back: Lying face down on a raft in your pool, slowly lift your upper body from the raft. Hold this position for the count of three and repeat.

Shoot Through: In the deep end of your pool, keep your body in an upright position and extend your arms straight out to your sides at shoulder height. Bring your knees toward your chest, then quickly press them to one side. Return to the center and press them toward the other side.

Suspended Exercises

Children must be able to tread water to perform these exercises, although the exercises can be done in shallow or deep water.

Kick the Seat in Front of You: Imagine you are sitting in a chair. You begin to kick the chair in front of you. See how long you can do this.

Imaginary Bicycle: Without touching the bottom of the pool, ride your imaginary bicycle around the pool. Go forward, backward, lean over, and bring your legs up to one side and then to the other side. Imagine you are riding uphill. Go as fast as you can. You can even race someone around your pool. For more of a challenge, try riding your bike with no hands—bring your hands up and out of the water!

Jumping Jacks: In the deep end of your pool, assume an upright position. Open your arms and legs to your sides. Immediately bring your body back to an upright position and repeat.

The Games Arranged
According to Group Size

Large Group

9. Racing Sea Rays
15. Fish and Net
19. Ship and Barnacles
21. Piranha Tag
22. Freeze Tag
23. Shark and Minnows
24. Bridges and Canals
35. Cannonball Contest
36. Underwater Bowling
50. The Toilet Flush
57. Dirty Backyard Cleanup
67. Take out the Garbage!
76. Shark Attack!
87. Seahorses and Mermaids
96. You've Got a Delivery

Any Size Group

37. Name the Jump
44. Weightless Challenge
73. Quick Draw

Even Number of Players

6. Car Tag
9. Racing Sea Rays
25. Snatch the Bait
48. Push 'Em Back
51. Steal the Bacon
52. Water-Balloon Volleyball
54. Baseball

55. Body Tug of War
56. Seahorse Toss
58. Underwater Rugby
57. Dirty Backyard Cleanup
62. Obstacle Course
63. Dodge the Sponge
64. Sponge Toss
67. Take out the Garbage
68. Basketball Bomb
69. Attack or Retreat
78. Blindfolded Guards
83. Jump Shot
85. Sponge Relay
86. Crossing the River
92. Over and Under
96. You've Got a Delivery
97. Best Friends
98. Back Me Up

2 or More Players

30. Underwater Race
33. Torpedo Ready
41. Long Jump
46. Sink the Sub
48. Push 'Em Back
82. Garden-Hose Limbo
84. Cruise Ship
88. Chase the Ball
89. Popcorn Races
100. The Kentucky Derby

3 or More Players

1. Follow the Leader
2. What Did You Say?
5. On with the Show
8. Jellyfish Bite
17. Marco Polo
27. Jump, You, Jump!
39. Pickle
93. Stinky Feet

4 or More Players

3. Spell It Out
4. What Am I?
11. Underwater Tag
13. Moby Dick
14. Elbow Tag
18. Pirate Treasure
20. Turtle Tag
25. Snatch the Bait
26. Limbo
28. Penny Hunt
29. Red Light, Green Light
31. Ducks and Sharks
32. Watermelon Race
34. Categories
38. La-La-La—Ahhhhh!
40. That's My Number
42. Below the Surface
43. Aqua Golf
45. Piñaqua
47. Underwater Leader
49. Message in the Bottle
52. Water-Balloon Volleyball
54. Baseball
55. Body Tug of War
58. Underwater Rugby
59. Octopus Race
60. Ping-Pong Scramble
61. Scavenger Hunt

62. Obstacle Course
63. Dodge the Sponge
64. Sponge Toss
65. Backseat Driver
66. Keep It Up
68. Basketball Bomb
69. Attack or Retreat
70. Basketball H_2O
71. Diving-Board Baseball
72. Hole in My Bucket
74. Splash
77. Pop-up
78. Blindfolded Guards
79. Graveyard
80. Pass the Sponge
81. Wash 'n' Run
83. Jump Shot
85. Sponge Relay
90. Hold My Baby, Please!
91. NASCAR Races
92. Over and Under
94. Tunnel Race
95. Wet T-Shirt Race
97. Best Friends
98. Back Me Up
99. Swimming Races
101. Pass and Shoot

6 or More Players

6. Car Tag
7. Lifeguard Tag
10. The Blob
12. Hook On
16. The King's Bridge
51. Steal the Bacon
53. To Catch a Thief
75. Cat and Mouse
86. Crossing the River

SmartFun *activity books encourage imagination, social interaction, and self-expression in children. Games are organized by the skills they develop, and simple icons indicate appropriate age levels, times of play, and group size. Most games are noncompetitive and require no special training. The series is widely used in schools, homes, and summer camps.*

101 RELAXATION GAMES FOR CHILDREN: Finding a Little Peace and Quiet In Between *by Allison Bartl*

The perfect antidote for unfocused and fidgety young children, these games help to maintain or restore order, refocus children's attention, and break up classroom routine. Most games are short and can be used as refreshers or treats. They lower noise levels in the classroom and help to make learning fun. **Ages 6 and up.**

>> 128 pages ... 96 illus. ... Paperback $14.95 ... Spiral bound $19.95

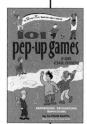

101 PEP-UP GAMES FOR CHILDREN: Refreshing, Recharging, Refocusing *by Allison Bartl*

Children get re-energized with these games! Designed for groups of mixed-age kids, the games require little or no preparation or props, with easier games toward the beginning and more advanced ones toward the end. All games are designed to help children release pent-up energy by getting them moving. **Ages 6–10.**

>> 128 pages ... 86 illus. ... Paperback $14.95 ... Spiral bound $19.95

101 QUICK-THINKING GAMES + RIDDLES FOR CHILDREN
by Allison Bartl

The 101 games and 65 riddles in this book will engage and delight students and bring fun into the classroom. All the games, puzzles, and riddles work with numbers and words, logic and reasoning, concentration and memory. Children use their thinking and math and verbal skills while they sing, clap, race, and read aloud. Certain games also allow kids to share their knowledge of songs, fairytales, and famous people. **Ages 6–10.**

>> 144 pages ... 95 illus. ... Paperback $14.95 ... Spiral bound $19.95

101 MOVEMENT GAMES FOR CHILDREN: Fun and Learning with Playful Movement *by Huberta Wiertsema*

Movement games help children develop sensory awareness and use movement for self-expression. The games are in sections including reaction games, cooperation games, and expression games, and feature old favorites such as Duck, Duck, Goose as well as new games such as Mirroring, Equal Pacing, and Moving Joints. **Ages 6 and up.**

>> 160 pages ... 49 illus. ... Paperback $14.95 ... Spiral bound $19.95

101 MUSIC GAMES FOR CHILDREN: Fun and Learning with Rhythm and Song *by Jerry Storms*

All you need to play these games are music CDs and simple instruments, many of which kids can make from common household items. Many games are good for large group settings, such as birthday parties, others are easily adapted to classroom needs. No musical knowledge is required. **Ages 4 and up.**

>> 160 pages ... 30 illus. ... Paperback $14.95 ... Spiral bound $19.95

101 MORE MUSIC GAMES FOR CHILDREN: New Fun and Learning with Rhythm and Song *by Jerry Storms*

This action-packed compendium offers musical activities that children can play while developing a love for music. Besides concentration and expression games, this book includes relaxation games, card and board games, and musical projects. **A multicultural section** includes songs and music from Mexico, Turkey, Surinam, Morocco, and the Middle East. **Ages 6 and up.**

>> 176 pages ... 78 illus. ... Paperback $14.95 ... Spiral bound $19.95

101 DANCE GAMES FOR CHILDREN: Fun and Creativity with Movement *by Paul Rooyackers*

These games encourage children to interact and express how they feel in creative ways, without words. They include meeting and greeting games, cooperation games, story dances, party dances, "musical puzzles," dances with props, and more. No dance training or athletic skills are required. **Ages 4 and up.**

>> 160 pages ... 36 illus. ... Paperback $14.95 ... Spiral bound $19.95

101 MORE DANCE GAMES FOR CHILDREN: New Fun and Creativity with Movement *by Paul Rooyackers*

Designed to help children develop spontaneity and cultural awareness, the games in this book include Animal Dances, Painting Dances, Dance Maps, and Story Dances. The **Dance Projects from Around the World** include Hula Dancing, Caribbean Carnival, Chinese Dragon Dance, and Capoeira. **Ages 4 and up.**

>> 176 pages ... 44 b/w photos. ... Paperback $14.95 ... Spiral bound $19.95

101 LANGUAGE GAMES FOR CHILDREN: Fun and Learning with Words, Stories and Poems *by Paul Rooyackers*

Language is perhaps the most important human skill, and play can make language more creative and memorable. The games in this book have been tested in classrooms around the world. They range from letter games to word play, story-writing, and poetry games, including Hidden Word and Haiku Arguments. **Ages 4 and up.**

>> 144 pages ... 27 illus. ... Paperback $14.95 ... Spiral bound $19.95

101 DRAMA GAMES FOR CHILDREN: Fun and Learning with Acting and Make-Believe *by Paul Rooyackers*

Drama games are a fun, dynamic form of play that help children explore their imagination and creativity. These noncompetitive games include introduction games, sensory games, pantomime games, story games, sound games, games with masks, games with costumes, and more. **Ages 4 and up.**

>> 160 pages ... 30 illus. ... Paperback $14.95 ... Spiral bound $19.95

101 MORE DRAMA GAMES FOR CHILDREN: New Fun and Learning with Acting and Make-Believe *by Paul Rooyackers*

These drama games require no acting skills — just an active imagination. The selection includes morphing games, observation games, dialog games, living video games, and game projects. **A special multicultural section** includes games on Greek drama, African storytelling, Southeast Asian puppetry, Pacific Northwest transformation masks, and Latino folk theater. **Ages 6 and up.**

>> 144 pages ... 35 illus. ... Paperback $14.95 ... Spiral bound $19.95

101 IMPROV GAMES FOR CHILDREN AND ADULTS
by Bob Bedore

Improv comedy offers the next step in drama and play: creating something out of nothing, reaching people using talents you don't know you possess. With exercises for teaching improv to children, advanced improv techniques, and tips for thinking on your feet — all from an acknowledged master of improv. **Ages 5 and up.**

>> 192 pages ... 65 b/w photos ... Paperback $14.95 ... Spiral bound $19.95

YOGA GAMES FOR CHILDREN: Fun and Fitness with Postures, Movements and Breath
by Danielle Bersma and Marjoke Visscher

A playful introduction to yoga, these games help young people develop body awareness, physical strength, and flexibility. The 54 activities are variations on traditional yoga exercises, clearly illustrated. Ideal for warm-ups and relaxing time-outs. **Ages 6–12.**

>> 160 pages ... 57 illus. ... Paperback $14.95 ... Spiral bound $19.95

THE YOGA ADVENTURE FOR CHILDREN: Playing, Dancing, Moving, Breathing, Relaxing *by Helen Purperhart*

Offers an opportunity for the whole family to laugh, play, and have fun together. This book explains yoga stretches and postures as well as the philosophy behind yoga. The exercises are good for a child's mental and physical development, and also improve concentration and self-esteem. **Ages 4–12.**

>> 144 pages ... 75 illus. ... Paperback $14.95 ... Spiral bound $19.95